KW-081-244

3 0116 01942411 6

# Prophetic Children

## Abraham Moses Jesus Mohammed

# Prophetic Children
## Abraham Moses Jesus Mohammed

Poems
**Fathieh Saudi**

Foreword by John Berger
Lotus Foundation

First published in the UK by The Lotus Foundation

www.lotusfoundation.org.uk


Book design by Fathieh Saudi

Drawings: Spiritual circles by Hana Saudi

Printed in Great Britain by Bell and Bain Ltd., Glasgow

ISBN 978-0-9559951-8-7

Copyright © 2012 by Fathieh Saudi


All rights reserved.


No part of this publication may be used or reproduced in any form or by any means without prior written permission of the author, except in the case of brief quotations embodied in articles and reviews.

# Contents

*To my father Abdel Majid Saudi, my*
*eternal friend through time, who*
*inspired my first line of poetry*

# A new voice

## Foreword by John Berger

This is a strange and haunting book. Not so much because of what it relates but because of its voice. I have not listened to such a voice before.

First there is the language chosen. Fathieh Saudi chose to write it in English, not in her mother tongue, which is Arabic. Her English is fluent but with an interesting foreign flavour in its repetitions, cadences and unexpected juxtaposition of terms, nouns, adjectives. Sailing on one sea, you feel the tides of an altogether other sea. And this carried me away!

Secondly - if we continue with the metaphor of a boat- there is the helmsman, the navigator, who is choosing the course. A woman, a woman of a certain age, but she is far more specific than that. She is writing about childhoods; Abraham, Moses, Jesus and Mohammed as small children. She is caring but not maternal; she is too complicit with the children to be a mother. Yet she knows the children intimately and physically. And she knows their mothers as well as she knows the boys. Who is she? The clue is that Fathieh Saudi was trained as a doctor, and then chose to practice in the Middle East as a paediatrician.

These four narrative poems are written by the hands of somebody with much experience of divining, soothing, alleviating the pains of children, and then of succouring them and making them smile.

Fathieh Saudi has translated the writings of Françoise Dalto into Arabic, and her poems here also make me think of the great English child psychiatrist Douglas Winnicott. Dalto, Winnicott and Saudi have the same modesty in face of the mystery of growing up. And in this clinical sense, each of them touches the prophetic.

The difference between them is that Saudi has an innate sense of poetry, of the healing power of words. And this, I imagine, derives from the written koranic tradition of classical Arabic. Words chant to her.

So much for the book's unique voice. What the voice tells of the four prophets' lives concerns their beginnings, concerns no more than the first biographical sentence of their lives. And within those distinct and different beginnings, it discovers and declares a similar experience of, or even identification with, pain, accompanied by a prophetic longing for peace and a vision of God.

"The love of God is pure," wrote Simone "Weil when both joy and suffering inspire an equal gratitude."[*]

Strangely and hauntingly, as I've said, this is a book which observes such a gratitude.

----

[*] Simone Weil *La Pesanteur et La Grace* p.75

14

# Abraham

I was conceived by the Euphrates.

Tera, my father, loved to pitch tent here, close to Ur.

My mother was deeply in love with him,

I could hear her chanting. Her laugh,

her joy, tasted like honey in the womb.

It was New Year.


From dawn to dusk, I could hear

tic - tic, toc - toc,

dom - dim, dom - dim,

rhythmic, regular beats.

I wondered if my father's heart was

as strong in the day as it was silent at night.

Ur was a wetland stretching
between Euphrates and Tigris: here palms
grew high, dates big as apples,
fields of barley reaching out of sight,
canals and streets crowded
day and night.

I grew up in a silent house.
My father spoke rarely. He seemed
so absorbed in shaping his stones,
melting mud and water,
engraving his sculptures.

*Each evening I heard my mother's prayers,*
*words recited, her legs crossed.*
*Each morning she bathed her gods,*
*fed them, dressed them, sang for them.*
*I couldn't grasp what hides behind it all.*

*Our home was filled with divinities*
*in marble, granite, clay,*
*stones of every colour. Many had faces,*
*some had wings, some life-sized,*
*others smiling. All*
*were my father's creation.*
*Nanna, god of the moon,*

*Nabu, the god of writing,*

*and hundreds more.*

*My father seemed to be blowing breath*

*into stone, unveiling the hidden life inside it.*

*As soon as a sculpture was finished,*

*he prostrates himself before his creation,*

*brought water and wine, meat and grains,*

*perfumes and camphor.*

*His creations seemed so lifeless to me. Were they*

*made from his tradition, love or fear?*

*Their touch was tender, soft,*

*yet they saddened my heart.*
*I wondered if they were so powerful to him or*
*he had projected his inner power onto them.*

*Few words passed between me and Tera.*
*Tenderness was not his way. I felt*
*I was absent to him, his endless creation*
*his only passion.*

*But I loved the evenings of Ur, listening to magical tales:*
*Eve and Adam, the flood, the kings of Uruk,*
*Gilgamesh my favourite of all; I felt so close to him,*
*his journey to a land at the ends of earth,*

a magical immortality moved my heart.
Could I succeed where he had failed?

Other stories troubled me:
the decline of Ur, of Sumerian culture,
the fear of an imminent disaster.

Tera was my master now, taught me
to sculpt the hardest stones, melt
 sand and water into brick, write
 in cuneiform, read ancient tales,
be a calligrapher on obelisks,
write poems for the gods.

*I excelled in all the art of Sumer,*

*I became a respected sculptor, engraver, poet.*


*Hundreds's of questions, hovering over my,*

*of metamorphosis, transformation,*

*yet I couldn't shape into words. Deities*

*frightened me, haunted my dreams,*

*tortured me. I couldn't adopt them as my gods.*

*Is my father the illusionist or Sumer's people?*


*Something I felt profoundly*

*beyond the earth, moon,*

*sky, the thousands of stars.*

*Death and the after - life tormented my being,*

*Though for the Sumerian there was no reincarnation,*

*no second life.*


*My adolescence felt miserable to me,*

*the air of Ur seemed oxygenless,*

*my chest contracted in pain,*

*nightmares invaded my day,*

*an expressionless mask covered my face.*

*I wished I could vanish.*


*One dawn I woke in the land of Harran.*

*I saw a deity stepping in the dark,*

*its silence turning to screams,*

*its arms reclaiming my life,*

*its hands becoming red-hot iron,*

*squeezing my neck.*


*I grasped my father's chisel, hammered*

*with all my strength, with all my hidden*

*anger, cracked the head of the biggest deity,*

*and it crumbled beneath my feet,*

*beheaded. I felt vertigo, a vast silence.*

*No one came to rescue it.*


*One dawn I saw an immense light*

from beyond the visible sky, God
spoke to me in dreams
and visions. I felt
like a feather, my heart
had been released, my mind
was crystal clear.

In that moment I was condemned by my father.
 I knew I had to run away
as far as my mind could go.
Ur ceased to be my city.
My father wasn't mine any more.
I couldn't face his eyes,

would have preferred me dead.

A voice was urging me to search through the invisible:

I wanted to reach the hidden truth about creation, life,

about human beings, non-human beings, death,

the vast universe.


My journey drove me to the Pharaoh's land,

I couldn't understand their

burial ceremonies, their obsession

with life after death. They were

stubborn, I couldn't speak

of my doubts or beliefs.

*My steps dragged me to the land of Canaan.*

*I adored the deep blue sky, the tender sea breeze,*

*the chant of the cogs at dawn, the smell of jasmine.*

*Their gods were more tolerant than Tera's:*

*Baal the highest God, El the supreme creator,*

*Anat the virgin. Sara*

*was my dear companion, my only beloved,*

*she excelled in reading my thoughts, my fears,*

*she was my saviour. She had to face abduction,*

*humiliation, to protect me. I owe her my life.*

*I could never oppose any of her wishes;*

*even when my heart broke into grains of sand,*

I had to surrender to her decisions.

One day Sara married me to Hagar, so as to have an heir.

Hagar lived between us for more than ten years,

I always felt she was a rebel Egyptian princess

not a slave as she pretended.

Hagar was a joy in my life, she gave me

my first son. I named him Ishmael, son from God.


Sara never accepted Ishmael as my son.

Jealousy scorched her heart. She became pregnant out of envy.

Isaac was born. Ishmael now ten years old.

Sara's heart was of basalt, I couldn't soften it,

she couldn't bear Isaac or Hagar.

Came the day when I had to expel Hagar and Ishmael into exile.

Ishmael, jewel of my eyes, was no longer around me.

I exiled both to the desert, to Mecca,

far from Ur, from Canaan,

I exiled a part of myself.

I the cruellest father on earth.


Isaac was strong, beautiful. I gave him my knowledge.

But a wall stretched more and more between us.

I am not the murderer of my sons, me

in the urge to scarify my son,

I am not a Cain.

A Sumerian would never sacrifice a living thing.

*Did my heart turn to stone*

*my consciousness abandon me?*

*It seemed as if I was testing the strength of my faith*

*if stronger than the life of my son. I was waiting*

*for God's intervention to rescue him. It felt as if*

*my consciousness was torturing me for exiling Ishmael.*

*Was my God testing my belief, my constant trust in him?*

*At Hagar's death, I travelled to Mecca.*

*Ishmael was beautiful, radiant as in his youth.*

*I felt he had a sword in his heart. He avoided me.*

*Nothing could repair the damage I had inflicted on him.*

One morning he announced the strangest wish,

to re-build a shrine in Mecca, the Ka'ba,

to install a meteoric stone in the centre.

I argued against it for hours.

Was my son holding onto that belief in deities from Tera,

my father whom I had forgotten for so long?

Ishmael yielded. We would not engrave on the shrine.


By my deathbed Isaac was there,

Ishmael was there.

Words were clear in my mind,

I felt identical love for both.

Ishmael, forgive my cruelty for exiling you, my elder son.

*Isaac, forgive my nightmare of sacrificing you, my younger son.*

*I wished that they would meet together somewhere.*


*O I could not utter a word.*

*Tears flowed with my almost last breath.*

*Would they hear my words now and in years to come?*

*Would they create a circle of compassion?*


*Life and death were twin in my life: each moment*

*I was living in one, I was at the door of the other,*

*life negotiated with death, death with life,*

*and I was living in between.*

*My journey was to fuse with the invisible,*

*to dig deep through doubt to certitude,*

*to harmonize the inner world and the outer,*

*how to surrender to death as to life.*


*I foresaw I would be revered by many faiths*

*yet to come. I would be their father, their guide,*

*their path to enlightenment. I was the first human to*

*open the way to God high high above.*

# Moses

*Echoing whispers burdened Yochebed's heart. I awoke*
*every day to the rhythm of her anxiety,*
*every night I shared her nightmares.*
*Confusion gripped my mind.*
*Why was she praying for me to be a girl?*

*The place of my birth was darkened at midday.*
*My mother held the veil between her lips.*
*Was she terrified by her own torments*
*or scared by the sound of my first breath?*

*Her nightmares grew ever more intense,*
*my innocent smile could not lessen them.*

Her troubled milk fed fear into my being.
Her heart released shivers into my body.
Did my death seem imminent to her?

The pharaoh saw in his dream a Hebrew child
dethrone him. He ordered his soldiers to raid
home after home, slaughter the firstborn boys.

One morning her milk tasted
of an unfamiliar serenity, her
hands warm and tender, her
smile angelic and wild. She
massaged my body with oil and camphor,
dressed me in blue velvet, hugged me

*tight for a second then laid me in a papyrus cradle,*

*covered me in blue silk, and set me adrift*

*through the reeds of the Nile.*


*There were no human sounds,*

*no heartbeats, no murmurs.*

*The water around me chilled my bones,*

*the turbulence nauseated me;*

*for the first time, I was desperate.*

*I drifted for hours and hours,*

*then the current turned to a stillness.*

Feeling bored, she walked the riverside,
the sand caressing her toes,
the wind blowing her hair.
"Is it a mermaid, a magic pearl,
a baby?" she wondered.

The darkness around me brightened,
the iciness turned to human warmth.
Had I been born again, in another womb?

I glimpsed a face glowing with wonder;
her arms were tender, her skin soft,
her heartbeat so steady, so rhythmic,
but I couldn't smell milk on her shawl.

*My being a boy didn't frighten her.*

*Her language was unfamiliar,*

*but she gave me my name. Moses:*

*The one drawn out of water.*


*I was adopted by this daughter of a king,*

*the one whose nights and dreams I disturbed.*

*I had already survived a second death.*

*I was only six months old. She*


*argued endlessly with her parents.*

*Only her tears stopped their shouting.*

*I felt she loved me deeply.*

I was crowned an Egyptian prince,

my home was a marble palace,

my clothes rainbows of colour,

my body scented with amber and sandalwood.

And a new destiny was mine.


Yet I never escaped those pounding feet,

the gallop of soldiers, swords piercing

children's bodies, babies drowned

in the Nile, the weep of unmothering

women never abandoned my dreams.

*Who am I to be to blame*

*for such tragedies? How much blood flowed*

*in place of mine? How many tears gushed*

*instead of my mother's?*

*I had forgotten about my mother for so long,*

*though still, each dusk, I missed*

*her heartbeats, their anarchy,*

*the scent of her milk.*

*Some nights I felt enraged, others*

*I felt grateful to her. Did she*

*hope to save my life or quell her fears?*

*Did she condemn me to life?*

*Did she condemn me to death?*

*I will never know. I will never know.*


*My eagerness to learn was infinite:*

*I mastered the wisdom of the Egyptians,*

*the mystery of hieroglyphs,*

*Assyrian literature, Chaldean astronomy,*

*excelled in all of them.*


*Yet each sunset strangeness overwhelmed me.*

*My only escape was the Nile.*

*I whispered stories of the river:*

watery rebirth, healing power, a journey to eternity.

Had I heard them in my mother's womb?


Neither the passage of years freed me, nor

the golden chains I wore.

My mood kept swinging

from compassion to violence

self-doubt to certainty,

kindness to rage.


I was strong as an eagle, yet my body

felt like ashes scattered across the world.

On oceans of thoughts, my mind never slept:

*am I an Egyptian prince,*

*a Hebrew slave,*

*the adopted child,*

*the abandoned one?*


*My heart was broken in two.*

*I had betrayed my poor mother,*

*and the pharaoh's daughter,*

*and my enslaved Hebrew tribe. Hadn't I?*


*The silence of my palace pulled me back*

*to the screams of babies dying instead of me.*

*My people's sweat, their sunburned faces,*

*their thin hands moulding mud and straw*
*brought back my mother's fears.*

*I was a prince who had become a wanted man,*
*condemned to death by my adopted father,*
*an exhausted stranger even to myself.*
*I felt exiled from myself and from*
*the universe around me.*

*Solitude was my only refuge*
*even when hundreds surrounded me.*
*I wished I could drown my memories,*
*myself. One dawn while the city,*

*the palace, my guards were still sleeping,*
*the sunrise seemed so familiar to me,*
*my steps darted ahead of my thoughts,*
*I would break free.*

*My long journey had begun. I would be*
*travelling to an unknown world,*
*reach Abyssinia, encounter Adoniah.*

*From exile to exile,*
*from city to wilderness,*
*I excelled in all states of exile.*

My journey lasted forty years.
One day I had reached Midian, the land of the Arabs.
Jethro, the healer, became my mentor; he offered me
his protection, a family of my own. He taught me
the art of being a shepherd, guided me
on my path. The wilderness became my home,
fig leaves my bed, Manna my food,
Mount Horeb my refuge.

My prophecy began.
I was in a new womb of bushes and fire.
I talked to God in thunder and lightning,
through whirlpools and rising pillars of mist.

I was free from the pharaoh's gods,
I had risen to the absolute oneness of God,
found the deep sense of free will,
a new vision of human justice.

From the heights of Nebo I glimpsed
the land of Canaan. A sensuous breeze
was soothing my heart.
I caught sight of the sea,
the green hills, peasants
 planting olive trees.
I wanted tokeep that vision
to the end of time.

I was one hundred and twenty,
the oldest traveller of mankind. I would
die soon in the heart of the wilderness,
though I longed to live forever.

I saw my solitary death. No one
would ever kneel before my grave.
No offerings, no sacrifices,
not even an engraved stone.

I tasted bitterness in my dreams.
My last breath abandoned me,
my soul continued to hold my body.

*My feeling of estrangement,*

*was suddenly swept away.*

*Homeland was a temple,*

*a pearl in the heart,*

*a vast world within.*

*I, exiled from birth to death,*

*had lived for so long to attain a state*

*of mind beyond consciousness, a continent*

*where no mere human being can go.*

# Jesus

*I knew the beauty of my mother,*

*like a butterfly with the wings of an eagle,*

*so young at my conception; her voice like a child's;*

*I loved the supple grace of her walk,*

*her laugh's resonance.*


*She prayed day and night in a temple,*

*her prayers soaked into my fragile skin,*

*I could smell the incense she offered to the gods.*

*I loved being in her womb. Calm, comforting.*

*She was still unmindful of my life.*

One midsummer night under a sky filled with stars,
Mary felt a life growing within.

*Suddenly my mother had stopped dancing, singing ,*
*even praying. Her hands were full of fear, her body*
*shrinking with me inside; wherever I turned*
*I felt her unease, heard her pain, her tears.*

*Her face had lost the brightness of its smile,*
*her pillow dampened by her tears,*
*my gentle kicks to comfort her in vain.*
*Was she drowning?*

Mary and Joseph shivered through each night, her sobbing

interlacing with his voice. As he

argued with her, she cried. To me,

he felt so old next to her.

His voice could comfort neither of us.


My mother became like an arched bow,

hugging her knees, curling in on her self,

me besieged. O mother

give me space to flow.


One morning we travelled for a whole day.

The words of Elizabeth my aunt were soothing:

*"You will give birth to a king-child,"*
*she whispered to my mother.*

*Her presence radiated peace.*
*She was pregnant too, "John*
*I will call him," she said.*
*With her baby, I felt intimate, identical.*
*We were already spiritual twins.*

*I loved Mary more with each new day,*
*yet couldn't comfort her nor hug her,*
*the taste of her sorrow filled my blood.*
*Her heart, full of tenderness, was my only escape,*

yet she had been running away since I was conceived.
From whom, for what, I didn't know.
Would my birth set her free?

My place of birth near the eastern slopes in Bethlehem
smelt strange, damp, of goats. The cold of the world
penetrated my fragile bones. I hoped
Mary would free me soon.

The moment of my birth I saw circles of light
around me. I felt so glad to be born,
as though I was on the top of the world.

*Mary's breasts were tender,*

*her milk like nourishing tears,*

*my attachment to her no language could explain.*

*She was my connection to the world, to the beyond.*

*I wished she would keep the cord between me and her.*


Night after night Herod's dreams haunted him:

a rebel is born, the king, the saviour. The slaughter

of all newborn boys. Night after night.


*Mary heard Joseph whispering about a predestined child.*

*Why should she be the mother for such a child,*

*she, desperate, with back pain and heartache?*

Joseph was blaming Mary for having a boy.

Palaces of rage in his mind, Joseph's eyes

frightened my heart. He and I

were like fire and oil each burning

the other as though I,

his son, was to blame.


Should he love me, save me, or hate me?

What to do with me, with Mary, with his life?

His voice reached me in the stillness of the night,

imploring the comets to show him the way,

neither the moonlight nor his wisdom

enough to guide him.

*One evening fearful whispers filled this world:*
*a slaughter of children had begun.*
*I sensed my father's nightmare,*
*tormenting his thought:*
*stop murdering all the babies.*
*The lamb you seek to hunt is mine.*

*I drowned in the anguish of Joseph.*
*Guilt and sorrow agonized his heart.*
*I heard the screams in his mind, of children*
*calling to him to save them, then*
*the silence of his dream.*

*I am no prophet to heal his nightmare.*

*One full moon night*
*I shared Joseph's new and tender dream:*
*Abraham was whispering into his heart to protect me,*
*then an angel calming the ocean of his tears.*

*That dawn I saw the eyes of Joseph full of tenderness.*
*His first fatherly hug lifted my heart like wings.*
*"Son, I promise you my protection, my love.*
*Your life will be a troubled journey."*
*I knew, at that moment, love*
*had been kindled in his heart.*

I murmured, "Joseph, be my father on earth. Love me."

A nourishing cord started to grow between us,

I forgot my troubled visions.

Why was I already giving him so much pain?

He was my saviour.


With the falling night, a new journey began. I was travelling

in a caravan. I loved the domed

sky, the warmth by the Nile,

I could count the stars one by one.

Peace dwelt between Mary and Joseph.

I felt free.

The time came to travel back to Nazareth,

return to Mary's home. I loved

watching the glimmers of the oil lamp,

goats and lambs feeding free in the fields,

the smell of stored wheat,

peasants planting grapevines,

valleys outstretching the horizon.


The rebel growing inside me was already adolescent.

My refuge was the Quarantal mountain,

 the caves of Qumran. Loneliness,

 anguish. Then light,

 enlightenment, wisdom.

*Forty days and nights, like months*

*extending into years, I talked and talked to*

*my loving, compassionate God.*


*I was eager to walk the whole earth.*

*My journey drew me to Tyre, Babylon, Byzantium, even India.*

*Some journeys were real, others miraculous through time and space.*


*I saw fear in the eyes of a lamb,*

*I listened to the alphabet of the wind,*

*I learned the language of birds,*

*I witnessed hope emerging from darkness,*

*I felt the mountain's silent whispering,*

I touched wordless souls,
I walked through time.
God whispered into the four
rooms of my heart.

I saw my prophecy.
Everything was so alive!
No creature should ever be sacrificed again,
"No more blood of any kind will run," I said.
"No more blood of any kind will run," I cried.

Amongst friends, neighbours, foreigners
I saw myself attaining a new dimension of knowledge,

67

*healing wounds, raising the dead . The only*
*wounded soul I couldn't heal was my own.*

*I foresaw my wings nailed,*
*my body stretched on a cross*
*my heart emptied of life.*
*Strangely I continued to breathe.*

*I sensed my followers would reach beyond my Hebrew tribe,*
*my name fill millions of hearts with love and tenderness.*
*Was that enough for me, wounded child as I was?*
*Was it enough to be blessed by the children who died for me?*

*My destiny was a burden for my beloved ones,*

*my followers, even for my beloved father.*

*Yet my journey was to put an end to suffering,*

*to liberate the soul, to reach another level*

*of consciousness. I started to love the music of that word.*


*Love was a flowing river in my life,*

*my disciples, my followers, Mary Magdalene,*

*Mary of Bethany, my mother. But I*

*was searching for the unique love of God,*

*the absolute.*


*On the Cross I could hear my heart*

whispering *"Eli, Eli, lama sabachthani"*
*"My God, My God, why have you forsaken me?"*
*God don't abandon me on the last day of my life.*
*God be my eternal father.*


*O God let me be the last to suffer on earth.*
*O God let me bring an end to anguish, pain, sorrow on the earth.*
*Let me be the last lamb to be sacrificed.*
*Let the world see infinite light through my soul.*

# Mohammed

I could taste salt on my lips.

Falling pearls were the first melody I heard.

Was it the fluid of the womb, or was it grief?


Amina, my mother, was mourning her beloved husband.

He had died on his way back home.

I will never see him. He will never hug me.


I missed the poems he had recited to my mother,

his whispers and laughs, his words

reaching me through her womb,

I felt I was floating in a wild cosmos,

in an ocean full of rhymes.

At my birth I was shamed by fatherlessness,
a first pearl of tear ran down my face.
I was grief.

I caught a glimpse of my mother's face,
her crown of sadness. I felt
she loved me. Did I remind her
of her lost beloved? She couldn't
feed me: her breasts were
engorged with tears.

My first journey took me to the desert.
I was breast-fed by an unknown woman.

Halima, my wet nurse, was so graceful,
her breasts abundant with milk. She recited
so many odes to me, lullabies, poems and songs.
She was the smiling image of my mother.

Halima was my first teacher:
she taught me the map of the stars,
how to build a tent and milk a goat.

Halima taught me to listen
to the whispering of the sand,
to the gusting of the wind,
how to mould mud into a home.

*Our nights were peopled with stories:*
*the sun mending broken hearts,*
*stray grains of sand returning home,*
*the moon delivering babies,*
*caves turning into palaces.*

*On my fourth birthday, I stopped needing Halima,*
*her care. It was time to come home.*

*My mother was still a widow.*
*The tears that had dried on her cheeks*
*persisted in her soul.*
*She had aged since my birth.*

*I felt powerless. I couldn't*

*name her sickness.*


*I wished I were an adult to ease her grief.*

*The rules of Quraish, our tribe, were strict:*

*a widow can't live on her own.*

*My uncle seemed so dominating.*

*I missed the enlightenment of Halima.*

*A rebel was starting to grow inside me.*


*My mother faded like a rose, day after day.*

*She died on my sixth birthday.*

*I was submerged by grief.*

*How many separations to come?*

*My grandfather reminded me of Halima*
*with his travelling tales to Petra, Basra, Palmyra.*
*The world seemed so vast. My dreams*
*were full of caravans, places,*
*languages. I cherished them all.*
*Can an orphan have such dreams?*

*Why had death come to me so often?*
*My father, my mother, my uncle,*
*then my grandfather, the most tragic of all.*
*His death broke my heart.*

*O death be my next journey,*

*let me join my beloved ones,*

*carry me with you.*

*I am already ten times an orphan.*


*One morning my uncle proclaimed*

*it was my time to enter manhood*

*with a long journey to Basra,*

*the city beautiful as in my dreams and even more so.*

*Here philosophers from five continents debated*

*the origin of the world, the universe, death and eternity.*


*Caravans were coming from India, Rome and distant China;*

Arabs, Hebrews and Romans discussed their scriptures;
scents of sandalwood and camphor mixed with
the perfumes of languages; musicians
played instruments I could not name. The world
had more meaning than ever before.

I loved sitting alone.
My presence radiated light, the monk Bouhira said.
He taught me all his knowledge:
creation, genesis, prophecy. "One day you
will become a prophet," he said.

The prophecy angered my uncle.

*I was taken back home that night with the first caravan.*

*"Light, prophecy, prophets, we don't need them,*

*Mecca is the centre of the world's creation,*

*our tribe worships hundreds of gods*

*like Aluzza, Allat, Hubal,*

*there is no room for one more idol,*

*no space for your One."*


*My only refuge was a cave called Hira.*

*Here the grains of sand and the wind*

*had mystical languages. Still*

*the light sat next to me,*

*brightening my inner being.*

*My mind was crystal clear.*

*The light one day spiralled itself, into words.*
*An angel appeared. Gabriel.*
*Wonderful words flowed from God,*
*a heavenly voice, drifting over me*
*like weightless feathers.*

*I had never heard such beauty before.*
*"Miracles are happening in my life," my heart whispered.*
*Who would believe in my prophecy ,*
*me, the illiterate orphan shepherd?*
*Where would I find a refuge?*

*Khadija, that night, cradled me like a baby,*

*covered my eyelids with tender kisses.*

*"You are a prophet," she said.*

*"I will be your first follower."*


*Eggs thrown into my face,*

*tomatoes staining the walls of my home,*

*swords flying over my body.*

*Rejection after rejection,*

*"You will die before becoming a prophet," my uncle had proclaimed.*

*"Become our king but never our prophet."*


*My journey into exile began,*

I travelled to Medina before dawn,

my disciples next to me.

The people of Medina were protective, provided us

with food, shelter, space to spread the message of God.


Here Gabriel instructed me to bow towards the Ka'aba,

site of the "Black Stone," meteorite on this earth

since Adam and Eve's fall.

Would Abraham and Ishmael return to life now?


God's holy message was already out of my hands.

The verses of Quran had dwelt deep

in the souls of my followers.

*I wasn't alone any more.*

*Death attended me again.*
*I lost Khadija, my first love,*
*my only woman for twenty-five years.*
*My children faded one after another.*
*O God let one of them live.*

*I, the orphan,*
*predestined to spread the grain of Islam,*
*my followers numbered thousands upon thousands.*
*I who had lost my family, my children, my beloved,*
*appointed to inhabit the hearts of millions.*

*I, the illiterate*
*I, who will die soon,*
*chosen to transmit a holy book,*
*a miraculous language.*

*Life is giving and receiving.*
*Life is receiving and giving.*
*Life is abundance and penury.*
*Life is penury and abundance.*

*Life is miraculous,*
*even for an orphan, an illiterate.*
*Life, the after-life, resurrection, eternity,*
*remain forever the mysterious enigma of my God.*

# Postscript
## by Fathieh Saudi

*I can travel back easily to all those wonderful summer evenings when I would sit on the balcony of our house in Amman, contemplating the transparent sky, the falling stars, the full moon, and the silence of the earth with a feeling of deep tranquility. Above all I remember sitting next to my father: his words were whispers touching my heart. I could hear the amazement in his voice at the splendour of God's creation: "God is love not fear". His words remain printed in my heart. Often in the mornings he would recite verses of the Quran with sincerity, rhythm and humility. Sometimes we would even talk about religion, creation, women's role, and society. Sometimes we didn't agree.*

*I remember also that during my childhood, we used to travel every Friday to Jerusalem. There I would walk through the narrow paved alleyways, coming upon mysterious places such as the   Dome of the Rock, from where* the Prophet Mohammed one night ascended to heaven to meet with Moses and Jesus. I would stand near the giant stones of the Lamentation Wall, where the Jews deposited folded letters containing their wishes in the hope that God would make them come true. And I would walk inside the Church of the Holy Sepulchre, full of scents and stained glass windows, built on the site of Jesus' crucifixion. Our miraculous journeys stopped after the Israeli-Arab war in 1967 and the occupation of west Jerusalem. My father passed away when I was only eighteen years old, but I think I kept his openness, his sense of awe at the universe, and his respect for other faiths.

Some ten years ago I came to live in London where I found myself confronted with one of the most traumatic periods of my own life. It was like being in the midst of a hurricane. I felt on the edge, in despair, uprooted, fragile, and exiled, as if disconnected from my whole past and even from my own language. And I wanted to find my way back to myself.

Fifty years had passed since my childhood. Unexpectedly I felt an urgent need to travel back to those times. My journey today has taken me to to *another dimension, symbolic, imaginative and poetical. My father is once more my guide; his photo, standing in silence on my desk, continues to send me love, warmth and trust in humanity.*

*I found myself on a path of re-discovery, about myself, my memories, my roots, the past and the meaning of my whole life. During this journey I was once more captivated by the prophets of my childhood: Abraham, Moses, Jesus and Mohammed. And I wanted to travel back to the prophets' childhoods, hoping to find a certain form of connectedness, comforting heritage; to relate present and past, and rediscover that mysterious feeling of wonder and trust. Living in London I was able to look at my childhood memories more profoundly and to relate them to the present.*

*My new journey took me, quite unexpectedly, closer to the suffering of each prophet during his childhood. Being trained as a paediatrician and working so closely with the newly born, and being convinced by the ideas of Francoise Dolto about the possible communication between a mother and her baby whilst in the womb, encouraged me to talk about the feelings and*

*emotions of babies and children. I realized that even prophets had*
*extremely painful childhoods, going through despair, rejection,*
*misunderstanding, identity crises, and humiliation imposed by those nearest*
*to them. In spite of that traumatic childhood, each prophet transcended his*
*suffering to find courage, rebellion, wisdom, generosity, abundance, love*
*for the creator, and a new religion which transformed the face of humanity.*

*Today I continue to be overwhelmed by my childhood visions about the*
*prophets and I feel the importance of understanding the continuity of and*
*the unity between the three faiths that share so much. Aren't they the three*
*main monotheistic religions and Abrahamic faiths? I feel that each prophet*
*holds a message of peace and justice that we need so much today in a world*
*where we are building walls of misunderstanding.*

*My poems find their inspiration in my own childhood, my adult sensibility,*
*my imagination, a poetic interpretation and a deeply mysterious call to*
*keep hold of hope and a positive interpretation of the world.*

# Acknowledgements

*I would like to express my heartfelt gratitude to many of my friends for their comments and advice on this collection. Their guidance, kindness, support and understanding will remain so precious and unforgettable all my life: Anne Rodford, Genie Lee, Jay Ramsay, Mona Saudi, Hana Saudi, Andrew Harvey, VA Harvey, Ursula James, Dia Batal, Sally Thompson, Graham Fawcett, Tania Naser, Anne Marie Teeowissen, Abdel ghani Abou Alazem, Faisal Darraj and Mahmoud Darwish.*

# About the author

Fathieh Saudi was born in Jordan. She completed her medical studies in France and worked as a paediatrician in Jordan and Lebanon, mainly with disadvantaged children. She has been involved for many years with the defence of human rights, peace and justice, particularly in the Middle East.

Over the last ten years, since moving to the UK, Saudi has been particularly interested in writing poetry as a means to express the interweaving between individual and collective issues and how we build our perception of the world around us; how, through our own personal path, we connect with a collective human language that aspires to the furtherance of justice and peace in the world. Saudi has also been concerned with interfaith and dialogue, the meaning of exile, women's creativity, literary translation and language.

Her poetry publications include *The Prophets: A poetic journey and River Daughter*, both in English, and *Bint Al-Naher* in Arabic. She has given poetry readings and performances in the United Kingdom and other countries.

Her previous publications include l'Oubli rebelle in French and *Days of Amber* in Arabic. She has translated several novels, poetry and scientific books from English and French into Arabic, including *La cause des enfants* by Francoise Dolto and *From A to X* by John Berger.

She is the recipient of several awards for her humanitarian and cultural work, including *Chevalier de l'Ordre du Merite* from France.